The True Story of LeBron James

Richard Barry

Minute Help Press

www.minutehelpguides.com

Table of Contents

Introduction

LeBron James is one of the most polarizing superstars of the NBA. His basketball career had a storybook beginning as he went straight from high school to the NBA's Cleveland Cavaliers, a team located close to his hometown of Akron, Ohio. After several years of contending for a title with the Cavs, but never winning it all, James made headlines around the world due to how he changed teams. Called "The Decision", James announced on live television with a special on ESPN that he was going to join the Miami Heat, in a move that many basketball fans saw as "cheating" or "poor sportsmanship." Since then, he has become both the most loved and most hated man in basketball. What caused such a dramatic shift in the public's view of this player? Perhaps a look at his life and career may provide some clues.

LeBron James: His Early Life and Childhood

Born December 30, 1984 in Akron, Ohio, LeBron Raymone James was raised by his mother, Gloria James. His childhood was not easy, as he didn't have a lot of stability and structure in his life. James said to ESPN The Magazine, "We moved from apartment to apartment, sometimes living with friends. My mom would always say, 'Don't get comfortable, because we may not be here long'."

James would head to the basketball court, making friends that he still has to this day, as well as developing his skills. Eventually James and his friends would form a basketball team that dominated in AAU play, under the instruction of Coach Dru Joyce. He wasn't "King James" during his childhood and middle school years, but he did rule over the basketball court. Often the biggest player for his team, he was also the player with the most skills.

The August 24, 1998 edition of The Cleveland Plain Dealer had a story about James and his team's success. The story said, "The Stars beat the Kenner (La.) Eagles, 53-36, for the 13-and-under title. LeBron James led the way with 21 points, Dru Joyce had nine and Jarrod Ferwerda scored eight". While he has yet to win a championship in the NBA, his early basketball career supplied many titles and plenty of awards and trophies.

In a 2010 interview with Larry King on CNN, filmed in Akron, James was asked about his childhood and his sporting prowess at a young age. He answered, "The first time on a basketball court was later on that year. Football season is always before basketball so I played in my first recreation league, I played for the Summit Lake Hornets, where I grew up playing basketball in 8-10 league. I was nine years old and we won the championship. I was one of the best players on the team back then so it was pretty fun. I was able to win a championship of football and basketball in the same year".

James also explained to Larry King about what life was like for him as a child in Akron. He said, "When I say, I didn't stay away from it, I didn't mean I was associated with gangs or I was associated with drugs. But when you live in the projects and you live in those circumstances there's nothing you can, you can't get away from it. But sports carried me away from being in a gang, or being associated with drugs. Sports was my way out".

Akron didn't have a team in the NBA (though many years earlier they were home to the Akron Wingfoots of the NBL), so when James was a child he had to look elsewhere for a basketball player to be inspired by. He was not a fan of the Cleveland Cavaliers, which in those days had stars Mark Price and Brad Daugherty, but never made it to the NBA Finals. Rather, he was a fan of the Chicago Bulls. Like many at that time, James chose Michael Jordan as someone to learn the game from and also as the reason for picking a jersey number, as James often wore the number 23. When interviewed for ESPN The Magazine, James said, "Got like 50 pictures of MJ on my wall, that's all you need to know about me".

More Than a Game: LeBron's High School Years

James played high school basketball for The Fighting Irish, at St. Vincent–St. Mary High School in Akron. How James plays the sport now in the NBA is similar to what he was doing in high school. LeBron James then, as he is now, was either too tall, too strong or too quick for who was guarding him, and often all three. One of James' unique highlight plays in the NBA is when he is a defender, running down someone who is on a fast break and swatting away their shot. James was doing that in high school games. His speed and control of the ball was also evident back in high school, as he could rebound the ball on the defensive glass and go coast to coast through the five players on the other team for the score.

The Cleveland Plain Dealer newspaper had a story about James on March 26, 2000. The story had the introduction, "When the lengthy postgame press conference was over, St. Vincent-St. Mary coach Keith Dambrot walked toward the locker room arm-in-arm with 6-4 freshman guard LeBron James. It resembled the final frames of a movie, when folks walk off into the sunset to greater things beyond the horizon". The team's coach was also quoted in the story and said, "LeBron is an intelligent kid" as well as "He can be as good as he wants to be". Obviously James wanted to be, and did become, a great player.

As he dominated high school basketball in his junior season there was talk that James and his mother would ask the NBA to change their rules, or take legal action, so he would be eligible to be drafted. The NBA wasn't going to allow a high school junior to enter the 2002 NBA Draft, but if it had happened it would have changed the NBA as James could have been drafted by the Rockets at pick 1, who picked Yao Ming, or the Bulls at pick 2 or Warriors at pick 3. While James was a megastar in Cleveland, if he could have joined Chicago for the 2002-03 season he would have followed in Michael Jordan's footsteps and also been on a team with Tyson Chandler and Eddy Curry, who were players that were drafted right out of high school.

Those basketball fans who didn't know about LeBron James were made aware of his potential when he was put on the cover of Sports Illustrated magazine. The February 2002 edition called him "The Chosen One" and also said "High school junior LeBron James would be an NBA lottery pick right now". Sports Illustrated also talked about LeBron James the previous year: in the July 23, 2001 issue his performance at the Adidas ABCD Camp was noted as he outplayed Lenny Cooke, who at the time was considered to be one of the top talents in high school basketball. ESPN The Magazine also had an article about LeBron in December of 2002. Tom Friend wrote about how big LeBron James was in high school basketball by going back two decades to the hype that the player who would later be known as Kareem Abdul-Jabbar had, "Not since Lew Alcindor has a high school senior been hoisted this high over the bean stalk, and there's an entire basketball public tripping all over itself in anticipation."

During LeBron's high school career there were times when he and those around him were investigated for accepting gifts. One of the most publicized controversies concerned a luxury Hummer SUV. The Ohio High School Athletic Association investigated how James was able to purchase the vehicle. Luckily for James he was not suspended from high school basketball, as his mother had financed the purchase through a bank loan. Accepting two sports jerseys from a store, reportedly uniforms of Wes Unseld and Gale Sayers, did get James into trouble with the OHSAA and threatened his high school eligibility, as James was suspended for several games.

An example of how rare a talent LeBron James was in high school was shown when ESPN broadcast a St. Vincent–St. Mary versus Oak Hill Academy game and used NBA Hall Of Famer Bill Walton and the legendary Dick Vitale to commentate, along with Dan Shulman. Vitale said before the game, "When you talk about LeBron James, it's been a runaway freight train". Vitale would also compare what James was doing at his young age with Tiger Woods, the Williams sisters and Alex Rodriguez. Courtside commentator Jay Bilas said, "LeBron James is the best high school basketball player I have ever seen." Bilas also compared James to Kobe Bryant at the same age, deciding that James was more advanced due to his size and passing ability.

If LeBron James ever wanted to play a second professional sport, he wouldn't try baseball like Jordan did, as James has the size and athleticism to be in the NFL. James played basketball and football in high school, and was First Team All-State for football in his sophomore season as a wide receiver. His basketball accolades in high school were much more impressive. James was Mr. Basketball for the state of Ohio three years in a row. He led St. Vincent-St. Mary High School to three state titles, was on the USA Today All-USA First Team three times, Gatorade Player of the Year twice and PARADE High School Boys Basketball Player of the Year two times.

In his first season of high school basketball, James averaged 18 points and 6 rebounds. He improved to 25 points and 7 rebounds as a sophomore. His numbers went up again as a junior, with averages of 29 points and 8 rebounds. He made his claim to be the top pick in the NBA Draft with senior season numbers of 32 points, 10 rebounds and 5 assists.

James was always going to the NBA but many wonder what would have happened if he did go to college, and where he would have attended. Schools that have been mentioned as being possibilities back then included Ohio State, Duke, Maryland, Louisville and North Carolina. Getting LeBron James could have meant a championship for any of those schools, especially Duke, as that year they were able to recruit the player considered to be one of the best out of high school, Luol Deng.

The film called More Than a Game shows the unique high school career that James had, as well as his friendships with teammates Sian Cotton, Dru Joyce III, Willie McGee and Romeo Travis. Those four would not get to the NBA although Romeo Travis did have a career playing basketball in international leagues. The Shooting Stars book, written by Buzz Bissinger with James, also covers his early life and the many years of basketball that this "Fab Five" played together.

James had a chance to showcase himself in front of NBA scouts and a large television audience when he played in the 2003 McDonald's High School All-American Game. James was the MVP of the game with 27 points on 12 for 24 shooting, and his versatility was on display with 7 assists and 7 rebounds. His teammates included point guard Chris Paul, a future NBA All-Star, and forward Charlie Villanueva, who would win a championship at NCAA level with UConn. Scoring 23 points for the West team was Shannon Brown, who would play three years of college basketball before being drafted by Cleveland in the NBA.

James had an alley-oop dunk on a pass from Chris Paul, and also set up his teammates in the same fashion in the 2003 McDonald's High School All-American Game. On a breakaway, James finished with a power dunk that was reminiscent of something Dominique Wilkins used to do. James also put on a display of highlights in the Powerade High School Jam Fest. Defeating Shannon Brown in the finals of the dunk competition, James was rocking the rim with his power dunks. He finished the competition by lobbing the ball from outside the court, the ball then bounced on the floor near the basket and James raced onto the court to catch the ball at the top of its bounce and slammed it home with a reverse, two-hand dunk.

While LeBron James would make a successful transition from high school to the NBA, others who played in the 2003 McDonald's High School All-American Game had different results after being drafted in the first round. Ndudi Ebi did little with Minnesota, Travis Outlaw developed into a solid scorer for Portland and Kendrick Perkins would later win the NBA title as the starting center of the Boston Celtics. LeBron James was on a different level to all the other star high school seniors of that year. He was listed at 240 pounds, so while he had skills to jump right to the NBA he was also ready physically. Forward Larry Bird played his NBA career at 220 pounds, shooting guard Michael Jordan was listed in the NBA at 216 pounds, and when power forward Karl Malone was dominating the NBA his weight was around 256 pounds. When LeBron James entered the NBA he did it with the skills of a guard, the height of a forward and the strength of more mature player. Presently his listed playing weight is 250 pounds, a mere 10 pounds over his high school weight.

Chosen One: His First Years with the Cleveland Cavaliers

One obstacle to LeBron James starting his NBA career in Ohio was the 2003 NBA Draft Lottery. The Cleveland Cavaliers did have the most chances, along with Denver, in the lottery, but the New York Knicks had a 1.5% shot at the top pick, the LA Clippers had an 8.9% chance and James' NBA career would have begun in Miami if the Heat had won the top pick when they had a 12% chance at it. Some of the other teams in the lottery included Toronto, Detroit and Chicago. Cleveland got what they wanted, as one of their 225 lottery combinations out of 1,000 was the right one and they landed the first overall selection.

Though for many in Cleveland the hometown hero LeBron James was the only choice, the Cavaliers did have other options at the top pick. Serbian prospect Darko Milicic went at pick two but had no chance at being selected at pick one, and Carmelo Anthony and Chris Bosh, who went at picks three and four, would also have been considered. In any other year, Carmelo Anthony would have been the top pick after he led Syracuse to the NCAA title and had a remarkable 20-10 average for the season. Bosh was a different type of prospect to James and Anthony: a very efficient scorer who had the potential to play all three frontline NBA positions.

Cleveland also had a pick early in the second round of that draft and seemed to make the right choice when they selected Jason Kapono. James could do everything on the court so he would need someone out there who could hit shots and that was Kapono's specialty. Kapono connected on 48% of his three-pointers in his rookie season but would then join the Bobcats in the 2004 NBA Expansion Draft.

James arrived with the Cavaliers and was immediately their best player. In the previous season the team was led in scoring by Ricky Davis. Zydrunas Ilgauskas had gotten over the foot problems he had earlier in his career and was an effective center. Carlos Boozer was a steal in the second round by the Cavs and they also had Dajuan Wagner, who the Cavs had drafted right out of high school with a lottery pick. The rest of the roster was full of journeymen.

How great a new player is for a team can be shown by the improvement in wins that the team has. Larry Bird, David Robinson and Tim Duncan lifted their teams to much better records in their rookie seasons, and when LeBron James joined the Cavs, who were coming off a season of only 17 wins, they improved to 35 wins for the 2003-04 season.

It didn't take long for Cleveland to figure out that Ricky Davis wasn't the right player to have next to James. Both players had similar games and needed the ball in their hands, but James was much better. During the season Davis was sent out in a trade package to Boston for center Tony Battie and forwards Eric Williams and Kedrick Brown. The Cavs also had Darius Miles, who was similar in some ways to James as he was a small forward and was drafted out of high school, and they traded him for point guard Jeff McInnis. McInnis provided outside shooting and also took some of the playmaking pressure off of James. Ira Newble was a valuable contributor who was signed as a free agent; he had the size to defend shooting guards and small forwards, which took some of the load off of James.

LeBron James' NBA career started with the Cavs in an away game at Sacramento, on October 29, 2003. James played 42 minutes but his 25 points and 9 assists was not enough to get Cleveland past a veteran Sacramento Kings team led by Peja Stojakovic, Vlade Divac and Mike Bibby. The final score was Sacramento 106 and Cleveland 92, but it was closer than the final score says as the Kings needed a big fourth quarter to seal the win.

The first home game in LeBron's career was against the Denver Nuggets, where basketball fans got to see the first NBA matchup of LeBron James and Carmelo Anthony. The Nuggets' new star had a solid game with 14 points and 6 rebounds, and Anthony's team won the game due to the strong play of Nene and Marcus Camby inside as well as the spark that little Earl Boykins provided off the bench with 18 points in 25 minutes. James didn't hit a lot of shots in the 93 to 89 loss, as he shot 3 for 11 from the field, but the crowd of 20,562 got to see his versatile game in action. James blocked 3 shots and had 2 steals, as well as 11 rebounds and 7 assists.

After five losses, James would record his first win in the NBA at home against the Washington Wizards. Playing 45 minutes, James led the way with 17 points, 8 rebounds and 9 assists. Washington had a combined 42 points from their high-powered backcourt of Gilbert Arenas and Larry Hughes but Cleveland got the victory, 111 to 98.

With per game averages for his first NBA season of more than 20 points, 5 rebounds and 5 assists, LeBron James proved he was able to play at the level that Oscar Robertson and Magic Johnson did. James was the obvious choice for the NBA's 2004 Rookie Of The Year, and out of 118 votes he received 78, with the other 40 going to Carmelo Anthony of the Denver Nuggets.

Success on the court for Cleveland was also matched by attendance numbers. The Cavs were getting an average of 11,496 fans to home games in the season before James arrived, and that number jumped to 18,287 for his rookie year.

It seemed that Cleveland had three key building blocks in place: superstar LeBron James at small forward, Zydrunas Ilgauskas at center and Carlos Boozer at power forward. That changed when Boozer left for the Utah Jazz as a free agent. While they would have been a much better team in the future if Boozer had stayed, Cleveland were able to fill the hole at power forward by trading with the Orlando Magic. The Cavs sent backup center Battie, as well as a couple of future second round picks to Orlando for power forward Drew Gooden and centers Anderson Varejao and Steven Hunter. Gooden would provide an offensive option, while Anderson Varejao was a steal by the Cavs as he quickly developed into an energy player who provided rebounds and blocks.

Cleveland also had a shot at drafting a sidekick for James. Jordan needed Pippen and Thomas needed Dumars, and with pick 10 in the 2004 NBA Draft Cleveland had their last shot at using a lottery pick to find the player that would combine with James to take the team to the top of the NBA. The draft wasn't loaded with talent, as Dwight Howard went with the first pick and there were no other prospects like him in that draft. Unfortunately, there were more future busts than stars. Andre Iguodala went at pick 9, and he would have been a good swingman to team with James, and at pick 10 the Cavs went with shooter Luke Jackson. A star for four seasons at Oregon, Jackson shot 44% on three-pointers in his senior season. He should have been the ideal player to spread the floor for the Cavs, but his game didn't work at the NBA level. Jackson never started a game for the Cavaliers and also battled injuries, and after two seasons he was traded away. Players who did become stars in the NBA who were drafted after pick 10 include Al Jefferson, Josh Smith, Jameer Nelson and Kevin Martin.

The Cavs did improve their roster for the 2004-05 season by trading for Eric Snow. The veteran point guard had been to the finals with the Philadelphia 76ers and knew how to defer to a superstar player, as Allen Iverson took all the shots for the 76ers. Snow wasn't a scorer, and didn't have the outside shot that the Cavs needed when James was double-teamed, but he was a leader on the floor who looked after the ball and played great defense. Shooter Sasha Pavlovic was acquired for a future draft pick.

Although James went very close to a triple-double in his rookie season, his first triple-double happened during the 2004-05 season. In January, the Cavaliers went to Portland and defeated the Trail Blazers 107 to 101. James played 44 minutes and produced 27 points, 11 rebounds and 10 assists. He had his shot going that game, hitting 11 of 16 shots, including a three-pointer. James didn't wait long to record his second career triple-double: two games later he had 28 points, 12 rebounds and 10 assists in a win at Golden State.

One team that James enjoyed playing against in 2004-05 season was the Toronto Raptors. James had 27 points and 10 assists the first time he played the Raptors during that season, and the second game was another win as James had 15 points, 8 rebounds and 11 assists. The only time the Raptors defeated the Cavs that year was in their third meeting, and it was close, with Toronto winning 105 to 98. It was still a special game for James, as he scored 56 points on March 20, 2005, an away game. Toronto's two best players that game were Jalen Rose and Donyell Marshall, and combined they only had 54 points. James was on fire like he had never been before in the NBA. His outside shot has always been inconsistent, but usually respectable, and in this game he hit 6 of 12 three-pointers. James has a career free throw percentage of around 75% but against the Raptors in this game he went to the line 15 times and only missed once. He still found his teammates as he passed for 5 assists, and he also worked on the glass for 10 rebounds.

From his first to his second season, James improved in nearly every statistical category. Two stats that he increased his numbers in were field goal percentage and points per game. James went from 41.7% from the field to 47.2%, while his scoring changed from 20.9 points per game to 27.2. His assists, steals and rebounds were up, while there was a slight drop in his turnovers per game.

Cleveland improved in 2004-05, but they did not make the playoffs. Coach Paul Silas didn't get to the end of the season as Brendan Malone took over. For the 2005-06 season, and for the rest of his time in Cleveland, James would be coached by Mike Brown.

Check My $tats: Lebron and the Cavs' Finally Enter the Playoffs

Unfortunately for Cleveland they did not have a selection in the 2005 NBA Draft. It had been traded away many years before, in a deal for shooter Wesley Person. If the Cavs had retained their pick in the 2005 NBA Draft they would have been in a position to draft Danny Granger. The Cavaliers did have money to spend and through free agency they tried to bring in the right mix of players to have around James.

A shooter was needed at the point guard spot, and with James handling the ball a lot it meant open shots and someone who was ready to take them and Damon Jones was signed for that role. Jones would share the point guard minutes with Eric Snow. Donyell Marshall was coming off a season when he went close to averaging a double-double while also hitting more than three three-pointers per game. He was signed to bring his versatile game off the bench in a 6th Man role for the Cavs.

Cleveland still had plenty of salary room as they hunted for the second star to put next to James. Milwaukee's Michael Redd would have been a great shooter to keep defenders from collapsing on James, but he stayed with the Bucks. Ray Allen, who was in Seattle at this time, could have been another option but Cleveland didn't get him. The Cavs settled on signing Larry Hughes, who was coming off a season averaging 22 points per game and nearly three steals per game. Cleveland made Hughes the highest-paid player on the team. Their investment didn't produce the expected results as Hughes averaged 15.5 points per game in his first season in Cleveland and his numbers would decrease in following seasons.

Meanwhile, James lifted his game to another level, averaging over 30 points per game, and Cleveland won 50 games for 2005-06 season. For extra offensive firepower, Cleveland brought in Ronald "Flip" Murray during the season. Following this, LeBron made the NBA Playoffs for the first time.

The first round opponent of Cleveland was the Washington Wizards. James lifted his scoring from 31.4 points per game during the regular season to 35.7 in this series. Washington couldn't contain James as he scored 32, 41, 45 and 32 points in Cleveland's wins, and the Cavs defeated the Wizards 4 games to 2.

Next up was the veteran Detroit Pistons team, with the Wallaces inside and Billups, Hamilton and Prince on the perimeter. The Pistons had too much experience but James and the Cavs pushed them to the limit as the series went the distance with Detroit winning 4 games to 3. James averaged 46 minutes per game in this series, and the only real rest he had was in Game 1, when he played 36 minutes in a blowout loss. His best game was his triple-double in the Game 3 win, where James had 21 points along with 10 rebounds, 10 assists and 4 steals.

James and the Cavs learned from their playoff loss to Detroit and hit the 2006-07 season with a determination to go deeper into the playoffs. Cleveland also kept most of their players, while adding draft picks Shannon Brown and Daniel Gibson, so that provided a sense of stability for the franchise.

With per game averages of 27.3 points, 6.7 rebounds and 6 assists, LeBron James led Cleveland to another 50-win season. The Cavs swept the Wizards in the first round, and in the second round it was Kidd, Carter, Jefferson and the rest of the New Jersey Nets. Cleveland won in six games, losing two games when James had his two lowest scores of the round, which were games of 18 and 20 points. The Cavs had a lot of confidence as they went into the next round and faced a rematch against the Pistons. It was a shock to many when James scored 10 points in Game 1 and 19 points in Game 2, and both were losses for Cleveland. Those were the only games that Cleveland would lose in the series: in the next four games James averaged over 30 points, including a huge game of 48 points in 50 minutes when Game 5 went into double overtime.

Many expected James to win a title in his fourth NBA season, as the young and athletic Cleveland team now faced the veteran San Antonio Spurs. When James scored 14 points on 4 of 16 shooting and had 6 turnovers in Game 1, it was clear that the Spurs had all the answers, as well as homecourt advantage. The Spurs would assign their defensive stopper Bruce Bowen to James. If James got past Bowen then Tim Duncan, who had 5 blocks in Game 1, was there to defend the basket.

What the Spurs had that James did not have on his team were three stars who could win games. San Antonio had Duncan dominating in the paint, point guard Tony Parker outplaying all the opponents the Cavs sent against him as well as Manu Ginobili, who was ready to hit key shots late in games. Something that was evident in many of his playoff series losses was that James might have been the best player on the floor, but the next three best players were on the other team.

James got a big, and deserved, pay rise for the 2007-08 season. What should have concerned Cleveland at the time was that James only added three years to his contract. The stability that the franchise had the previous season was not there in 2007-08, and after going through several losing streaks the team was blown up midseason. James was still doing everything, including leading the NBA for the season with an average of 30 points per game, but his supporting cast was considered to not be up to the required standard.

Cleveland brought in Chicago and Seattle and they agreed on a blockbuster trade. Larry Hughes, Drew Gooden and Donyell Marshall were some of the Cavs that departed. Something that Cleveland never had enough of around James was outside shooting, so they acquired Wally Szczerbiak and Delonte West. Defense and experience were the attributes that Ben Wallace and Joe Smith were expected to bring to the Cavs.

The Cavaliers did win 45 games in 2007-08, but again a lot of the work was left to James, with Zydrunas Ilgauskas still the second best option on the team. The highlight of James' regular season was a visit to New York, scoring 50 points against the Knicks.

If the Cavs were going to get back to the NBA Finals they needed to hit the playoffs with momentum, but that didn't happen as they had a three-game losing streak in late March and a .500 record for April. Cleveland managed to get by the Wizards in the first round, with James averaging around 30 points per game and closing out the series with a triple-double, and then faced Boston in the next round.

The importance of homecourt advantage was evident as Cleveland won when playing at home but lost all four games in Boston. James also saw how three superstars and a veteran group of role players alongside them could take a team to the championship. It certainly wasn't James' fault that Cleveland lost Game 7. James scored 45 points as he and Paul Pierce, who had 41 points for the game, had a shootout like Bird and Wilkins did many years earlier in the same city.

James may have been the best player in the series, but the Celtics had Pierce, Ray Allen and Kevin Garnett. Boston also had veteran defender James Posey to use against James, big-men Kendrick Perkins and PJ Brown to make it difficult for Ilgauskas, and while the Cavs had traded away draft picks or selected the wrong players the Celtics had Rajon Rondo, who was a steal in the middle of the draft.

It was another playoff loss for James but he had something else to fill in his summer during 2008; the Olympic Games in Beijing, China. The run to the Gold Medal showed James what could have been and also what was possible in the future. Former Cav Carlos Boozer was on the roster as well as Michael Redd, who was close to being acquired by Cleveland. Of course basketball fans now can look back and see that James was on the same team as Dwyane Wade and Chris Bosh. Those two didn't even start in the final game; the team was so deep that James was on the floor with Jason Kidd and Kobe Bryant at guard, Carmelo Anthony at forward and Dwight Howard at center. James had previously won two Bronze Medals, at the 2004 Olympics and the 2006 World Championships.

For 2008-09 season, James had yet another new running mate on the Cavs. Mo Williams was brought in to handle the point guard duties and to hit big shots. Williams had been a late draft pick by Utah, and after a season with the Jazz he signed with the Milwaukee Bucks and had developed into a player that could average 17 points per game. It didn't cost Cleveland a lot to land Williams via trade, just Damon Jones and Joe Smith, and Williams would also provide something special in the future for Cleveland when he would later be traded for a future draft pick that would end up being the top pick.

James started the season with a game in Boston, where he scored 22 points and the Celtics won, but after that the Cavs hit top gear and ended up with a record of 66 wins and 16 losses. James once again played like a superstar, Williams was a useful second option, Ilgauskas and Varejao were getting the job done in the paint while West and Gibson provided the required outside shooting.

With regular season averages of 28.4 points, 7.6 rebounds and 7.2 assists, LeBron James had another great season. The postseason got off to a good start as Cleveland got the brooms out as the Cavs swept the Pistons in the first round as well as the Atlanta Hawks in the second. Cleveland just needed to defeat Orlando and James would have been back in the NBA Finals, but when he scored 49 points in Game 1 and it wasn't enough to get the win, the scene was set for another disappointment in the playoffs. Cleveland went out in six games, and as Dwight Howard scored 40 points in the last game of the series it showed Cleveland that they needed more size inside to compete.

Quitness: LeBron's Final Season with the Cleveland Cavaliers

The 2009-10 season would be the last for James in Cleveland. The Cavaliers wanted to convince him to stay, and management went out and got someone they thought could help the team win, which would be a reason for James to sign a new contract. Out went Ben Wallace, who had not been a good fit, as well as Sasha Pavlovic, some money and a future second round pick. In for Cleveland was someone who had won titles beside Kobe Bryant and Dwyane Wade, and nearly won it all with Penny Hardaway: LeBron James now had Shaquille O'Neal on his team. Free agent shooting guard Anthony Parker was also added.

It was a very different type of basketball season for James. His team was successful with 61 wins, but it was also developing into a circus, as many stops in other cities were turning into a recruitment process. One team that was looking to have money to spend for free agents in the summer of 2010 was the New York Knicks. James scored 33 points as Cleveland won 100 to 91, but the fans at Madison Square Garden didn't really mind as they thought it was a preview of a player they would have on their team a year later.

There were many teams that not only wanted James as a free agent but also would be able to configure their salary cap to be able to sign him, and James put on a show whenever he visited during the season. James scored 32 points, as did Wade for the Heat, as Cleveland won a close game in Miami. Twenty-six points and 14 rebounds from James were the numbers he had in a big win in New Jersey.

James and Cleveland were winning but there was still the idea that another piece was needed. Using the expiring contract of Ilgauskas, as well as a first round pick, Cleveland brought in forward Antawn Jamison from Washington. Cleveland were opening the bank as taking on the remaining years of Jamison's deal was the real price for the franchise. Washington would waive Ilgauskas and a month later he would be back with the Cavs.

With season averages of 29.7 points, 7.3 rebounds and 8.6 assists, James would win his second MVP award in a row. Both times he would receive nearly all the first place votes. When he won the 2008-09 MVP it was Bryant and Wade who were far away in second and third place. For 2009-10, James picked up 116 first place votes and the only others to get any were Kevin Durant with 4 first place votes and Dwight Howard with 3 first place votes. Some of the other NBA superstars to have consecutive MVP Awards in recent years are Steve Nash, Tim Duncan, Michael Jordan, Magic Johnson, Larry Bird and Moses Malone.

There was never a problem with winning regular season games for James, it was the playoffs that mattered. In the first round it was the Chicago Bulls. Cleveland won the first game with everyone contributing: James scored 24 points while Jamison had a double-double and Mo Williams had 19 points and 10 assists against Derrick Rose. James turned it on in the second game of the series as Cleveland won due to his 40 points. The series moved to Chicago and despite 39 points from James it was a loss for Cleveland. The next game was a huge win to the Cavs as James had a triple-double with 37 points, 12 rebounds and 11 assists. Cleveland would win the series in five games.

Once again it was LeBron James and Cleveland against the Boston Celtics, the best player in the NBA versus a team that could put four stars on the floor. Cleveland split the first two games of the series with James scoring 35 points in a win and then 24 points in a loss. Game 3 could have been the defining moment of the series as Cleveland went into Boston and behind James' 38 points on 14 of 22 shooting the Cavs won the game 124 to 95. Not only did James dominate but all the other starters scored in double-figures for the Cavs while the bench also made important contributions. Cleveland had managed to limit Paul Pierce and Ray Allen to a combined total of 18 points.

While the first three games of the series were very good for James and the Cavs, the last three were a disaster. James averaged 32.3 points per game and shot the ball very well early in the series but then everything turned around. Game 4 was a loss for Cleveland as James turned the ball over seven times and only hit 7 of 18 shots from the field. With the series tied at two games each, the pivotal Game 5 would be one of the worst NBA games that James would ever play. This was when people started wondering if James had quit on Cleveland. He scored 15 points, shooting 3 for 14. Boston won 122 to 88 and the series moved back to Boston. James ended his career with the Cavs by bringing in another triple-double, but he also had 9 turnovers and only hit 8 of 21 shots as they were eliminated.

During his seven years with the Cleveland Cavaliers, James had turned around a franchise that was at the bottom of the standings and made them a contender. James also increased the value of the franchise and helped fill the seats in the building. A regular in the annual All-Star Game, James was the MVP of the event two times. Except for one game in the 2007-08 season when he came off the bench against Indiana as he had just returned from injury, James started every game he played for Cleveland. When he played, Cleveland could not only expect a win but also for James to get around 30 points, 7 rebounds and 7 assists. James' contract expired after the 2009-10 season and he had a decision to make: stay with the Cavs or find a new team.

Taking His Talents to South Beach: LeBron James, Free Agency and Signing with the Miami Heat

Before "The Decision", NBA teams had to get into a financial position to be able to offer LeBron James a contract. Under the NBA rules, Cleveland were able to give James a maximum-contract even though they were over the cap, but for the other teams that wanted James they needed to create room. New York often looked like the favorite among the teams chasing LeBron, especially as he was often seen wearing a Yankees cap. The Knicks did everything they could to clear enough space to sign James and another top superstar. When they traded prospect Jordan Hill and future draft choices to clear out the contract of Jared Jeffries it looked like James and someone like Chris Bosh would be signing with the Knicks.

Another team that thought they had plenty to offer James, as they would also be playing in New York City a couple of years later and had room to sign him, was New Jersey. Brook Lopez was a young center on the Nets and they also had a high draft choice to bring in another prospect. Devin Harris was a star point guard who would be able to get James the ball if he joined New Jersey. As teams became desperate to create more space for free agents, the Nets were able to move out Yi Jianlian and his contract.

Chicago also had space in their cap, a young center in Joakim Noah and a star point guard in Derrick Rose. The Bulls hoped that James would want to follow Jordan and win with the Bulls. Chicago made a huge move around the time of the 2010 NBA Draft as they moved out Kirk Hinrich's contract by sending him to Washington along with Kevin Seraphin, a player the Bulls had selected in the first round, to create even more room to sign free agents.

The Heat also announced their intention to bring in two superstar free agents as they worked hard to create space in their salary cap. Nearly everyone on their roster had an expiring contract, with Jermaine O'Neal's ending deal creating a lot of space. Miami were worried they needed more money so they used their imagination. Daequan Cook was a streaky shooter but when he was hitting three-pointers it could change a game. Miami sent Cook and a first round pick to Oklahoma City; they only got back a second rounder but had moved out a contract. Michael Beasley was supposed to be a key part of the Heat after they used the second overall pick in the 2008 NBA Draft to select him, but a shot at signing James made Beasley expendable and they were able to send him to the Minnesota Timberwolves in a deal that did not bring a player who was under contract back.

A team that was thought to have an outside chance at securing LeBron James was the LA Clippers. They had enough money to sign James and a big hole at small forward to fill. James would also be joining a solid group of players as the Clippers had Baron Davis at the point, Chris Kamen at center and young shooting guard Eric Gordon. What the Clippers hoped would get James to consider them was the unique setting of playing basketball in LA, to battle Kobe Bryant and the Lakers for the city, as well as the opportunity to play next to exciting rookie Blake Griffin.

Cleveland had a lot of competition to keep James. They also had few ways to improve the team as they had traded draft picks and spent money to bring in veterans. What they did have was James' connection to the city and the state of Ohio. All the teams that James was interested in signing with had meetings with James but would have to wait for his announcement. James wasn't going to announce if he was staying in Cleveland or joining a new team in the usual way: he was going to have a one hour special on ESPN. "The Decision" would be one of the most controversial moments of his career.

Broadcast live around the world, the show was filmed at a Boys & Girls Club in Greenwich, Connecticut and was hosted by Jim Gray. From ESPN's transcript of the show, James announced who he would play for when he said, "In this fall, this is very tough, in this fall I'm going to take my talents to South Beach and join the Miami Heat". The news was met with excitement in Miami, other cities that were in the running to bring him in were not impressed, and Cleveland was devastated. Following The Decision fans in Cleveland burned their LeBron James jerseys in bonfires.

James arrived in Miami and along with Chris Bosh and Dwyane Wade the Heat had a party celebrating the new team of superstars. For the teams and fans that missed out on signing the free agents the party was just as unpopular as James' announcement of which team he was going to. With a band, smoke, a giant screen and fire shooting out of the stage, James, Bosh and Wade were introduced to the crowd of Heat fans. The three players then sat on chairs and said what they intended to do that season. When asked how many championships they would win, James replied "Not two, not three, not four, not five, not six, not seven", setting the bar very high for what was expected.

Pat Riley, who had previously built Miami teams around Alonzo Mourning and Tim Hardaway and then won a championship with Shaquille O'Neal and Dwyane Wade, still had a lot of work to do as the Heat had their "Big Three" but only point guard Mario Chalmers as well, and needed to fill their roster.

Miami gave a new contract to Udonis Haslem, the veteran had played several seasons with the Heat and was used as a power forward and center. Next for the Heat was the signing of another free agent that many teams were chasing, Mike Miller. He was brought in to provide outside shooting, and James Jones and Eddie House were also signed for their ability to hit the outside shot. Carlos Arroyo was brought in as a veteran to play the point guard spot. James can do everything on the basketball court except play the center position, so the Heat signed Joel Anthony, Jamaal Magloire and Juwan Howard to patrol the paint and also added former Cleveland center Zydrunas Ilgauskas.

A schedule that LeBron James was familiar with, he and the Heat played their first game of the regular season at Boston. James was ready for the big game and responded with 31 points, including hitting 3 of 6 three-pointers. Bosh only had 8 points and Wade, who had missed time in preseason due to injury and wasn't at his best, had 13 points. Boston won 88 to 80 but Miami would win their next four games to get their season off to a good start.

December 2, 2010 was a date that Cleveland fans had circled on their calendars, as this was the first time James would play in Cleveland on a team other than the Cavs. A crowd of 20,562 watched as Cleveland struggled and James and the Heat won 118 to 90. Except for guard Daniel Gibson who hit 4 three-pointers, Cleveland couldn't compete. James Jones hit 5 three-pointers for Miami and all three of their superstars played well. Dwyane Wade had 22 points, 9 rebounds and 9 assists while Chris Bosh hit 6 of his 11 shots for 15 points. James only played 30 minutes, scored 38 points and didn't have a single turnover. He shot 15 of 25 from the field, passed for 8 assists, brought down 5 rebounds and added a steal and a block.

The Heat were winning most of their games but did lose three games in a row during November. That was quickly forgotten as James and the Heat hardly lost a game in December. The winning streak also included a visit to New York, whose fans were not as welcoming as they were in his last season for Cleveland, and James had a triple-double with 32 points, 11 rebounds and 10 assists.

In January, James missed two games with an ankle problem and the Heat lost both of them, as they lost five of six games. Miami had a big win against Orlando early in February, with LeBron scoring 51 points, shooting 68% from the field. But late February and early March was another bad stretch for the Heat, and their losing streak was made worse when Coach Erik Spoelstra announced that some of the Miami players were crying after a close loss.

After five losses in a row, the Heat had a season-defining game coming up as Kobe Bryant and the Lakers were visiting Miami. Bryant scored 24 points, on 8 for 21 shooting, and Pau Gasol added 20 points but it wasn't enough as the Heat bounced back for a 94 to 88 win. Bosh scored 24 points and Wade had 20. LeBron James was the difference as he had 19 points, 8 rebounds and 9 assists. From that moment, the Heat won nearly all the games they played.

The 2011 NBA All-Star Game provided James with another opportunity to show his ability on the basketball court, but the East team was an interesting mix of players he could have signed to play with, as well as some of his fiercest rivals. James was voted in as a starter, as was Wade, and the other starters were Dwight Howard, Amare Stoudemire and Derrick Rose. The Knicks had cleared room to sign both Stoudemire and James but James didn't choose them. Chicago also created space to sign James, and the chance to have eventual 2011 NBA MVP Rose creating shots for him, but James spurned them as well. While Chris Bosh was added to the bench for the All-Star team, four Celtics who had defeated him in the playoffs were there as well, with Pierce, Garnett, Allen and Rondo. James had a triple-double in the game with 29 points, 12 rebounds and 10 assists.

With trades and free agent signings, several of the contending teams were looking to improve their rosters and improve their chances against the Heat in the playoffs. When Mike Bibby was traded from Atlanta to Washington it created a scenario where the Heat had a chance to add a veteran at point guard who had been in a lot of playoff battles in his career. The Wizards would come to an agreement to release Bibby from his contract, Miami created a roster spot by waiving Carlos Arroyo and then Bibby signed with the Heat. Bibby's outside shot was needed by Miami as Mike Miller missed a lot of games due to injury.

Cleveland fans that circled March 29, 2011 on their calendars may have been expecting another big loss to James and his new team. The Cavs were down at the bottom of the standings, while the Heat had won nine of their last ten games, which included a game against San Antonio where Miami won by 30 points. James, Wade and Bibby combined for 74 points but the rest of the Miami team only had 16 points as Bosh had 10 while off the bench Howard scored 4 points and Jones 2 points. James had a triple-double as he added 10 rebounds and 12 assists to his 27 points but Cleveland upset Miami 102 to 90. Baron Davis had 7 assists and hit two important three-pointers. J.J. Hickson and Ryan Hollins dominated inside while Cleveland also had solid contributors off the bench in Ramon Sessions, Luke Harangody and Christian Eyenga.

The loss at Cleveland was a minor bump on the road to the playoffs for LeBron James and the Heat, as they would only lose one more game, this time against the Bucks, in the regular season. A 100 to 77 victory over the Boston Celtics helped the Heat move above them in the standings to ensure James would not have to play a potential Game 7 in Boston.

James shot 51% from the field during the regular season. He scored 26.7 points per game to lead the Heat. James also provided 7.5 rebounds, 7 assists and 1.6 steals per game. James only missed three games, which included the final game of the regular season against the Raptors when playoff spots were set so Miami rested their three superstars. With 58 wins the Miami Heat won the Southeast Division and headed to the playoffs with a lot of confidence.

From "We Da Bess" to "How My Dirk Taste?" LeBron James, the Playoffs and 2011 NBA Finals Against the Dallas Mavericks

The first round of the playoffs was supposed to be easy for Miami. The Philadelphia 76ers only had a 41 and 41 record for the season and many thought they had overachieved as Coach Doug Collins tried to combine veterans like Elton Brand and Andre Iguodala with young players Jrue Holiday and Evan Turner. Miami won their first two games and then were off to Philadelphia, hoping to wrap up the series. James scored 24 points and added 15 rebounds and 6 assists as Miami had a narrow victory in Game 3, 100 to 94. In the next game, 31 points from LeBron wasn't enough to finish off the 76ers as Lou Williams and Turner both came off the bench for 17 points. It was a brief setback, but Miami went back home and won the series with a 97 to 91 victory.

James was going to have to go through the Celtics, the Heat's round two opponents, once again in the playoffs. It seemed to be a different story this time as the Heat won the first two games at home. James had 22 points in the first game and 35 points, on 14 of 25 shooting from the field, in the second. Miami could end the series in Boston, although winning one of the two games would be enough to maintain their advantage. In Game 3, it was a familiar experience for James as the Celtics kept him contained, and he scored only 15 points. A famous incident from the game was Wade fouling Rajon Rondo, and while Rondo would return to the game he would be restricted for the remainder of the series due to his elbow injury. Game 4 was the win that James needed, as he took care of business with 35 points and 14 rebounds. A 97 to 87 victory in Game 5 eliminated the Celtics and moved the Heat one step closer to the championship.

The Miami Heat are built around James, Wade and Bosh, which leaves two other spots on the floor as the weak points. During the 2010-11 season the Heat lost a number of games when superstar point guards were impossible to stop. Rose, Paul, Williams, Rondo and others were able to take over games. To get to the 2011 NBA Finals, the Heat needed to find a way to slow down MVP Derrick Rose. Chicago's big and very active center Noah was also a potential problem for the Heat.

Miami started the series with a loss. James could only score 15 points, in one of his most inaccurate games of the season he hit only 5 of 15 shots. Bibby and Chalmers were no match for Rose and the Chicago star scored 28 points. Joakim Noah produced 14 rebounds and 2 blocks. To avoid another playoff disaster, James was going to need to turn it on, and he did.

Game 2 was very different for James as his shot was on. He took 21 shots and hit 12, which equalled a shooting percentage of 57.1%. Seeing Noah and Boozer control the glass in the first game, James helped the Heat win with 10 rebounds. James hit a couple of three-pointers, stole the ball three times and the Heat won 85 to 75.

The next three games of the series saw James bring in some phenomenal numbers. He would hit his free throws at 94%, and was getting to the foul line a lot. James was scoring and also getting the Bulls into foul trouble. James had at least 2 steals and 2 blocks in each of the three games. In Game 3 he had 10 assists and in Game 5 he had 11 rebounds. The Heat won the series and were in the NBA Finals, just as they had predicted before the season started.

James and the Heat may have been expecting to meet the LA Lakers in the championship decider. San Antonio and Oklahoma City were other possibilities. Instead it was the Dallas Mavericks, the same team that Miami had defeated in 2006 to win their first championship. Miami were confident as they had homecourt advantage and Dallas were missing one of their better players, small forward Caron Butler, who was injured.

After years of being the sole superstar on a team that was playing against three superstars, James now had the chance to be on the side with the three superstars. It was James, Wade and Bosh against Dirk Nowitzki. In Game 1, it was just like the times when James played for the Cavs and lost to the Celtics, but the roles were reversed and now James was on the winning side. Dirk Nowitzki scored 27 points and may have been the best player on the court, but his team lost and the next best players were all from the Heat. James scored 24 points, and surprised with 4 three-pointers, while Wade had 22 points and Bosh 19 points.

James was now three wins away from his first NBA title. In Game 2 James scored 20 points and added 8 rebounds, 4 assists and 4 steals, Dwyane Wade exploded for 36 points, Miami had a large lead in the fourth quarter, and somehow they lost. While Dirk Nowitzki was a big reason why the Mavs won, several reasons why the Heat lost were the point guard and center spots and the benches. Both teams could put defenders at the center position, but Dallas also had 13 points from Tyson Chandler while the Heat's Joel Anthony went scoreless, although he did have 3 blocks, and Udonis Haslem could only manage 2 points in 29 minutes. At point guard, Bibby hit 4 three-pointers but couldn't get a single assist and Chalmers didn't have his shot going. Jason Kidd and Jose Juan Barea made some key plays for Dallas but it was guard Jason Terry who was the difference between the teams. One thing the Heat didn't have was a spark off the bench, like "The Microwave" Vinnie Johnson used to be for the Pistons, but that is what Dallas had with Jason "JET" Terry. He came off the bench for 16 points, 5 assists and 2 steals, and Dallas had evened the series.

Game 3 in Dallas was a win to the Heat, 88 to 86. James had 17 points and 9 assists. Everything seemed to be back on track for the Heat, but instead it was the beginning of the end of their season. Dallas had a plan: make James and Wade jump shooters. It worked in Game 4 as James shot 3 for 11. In Game 5 James had a triple-double but his shooting was still off, at 8 for 19. Miami looked beaten and Dallas were confident as the series moved back to Florida. Many were saying that James didn't perform in the important fourth quarters.

Jason Terry came off the Dallas bench for 27 points, Nowitzki added 21 points and 11 rebounds, DeShawn Stevenson hit important outside shots, hard-working Brian Cardinal contributed hustle plays, Barea was too quick, Marion made it difficult for LeBron James and Dallas was too deep and too good. The Mavericks won 105 to 95. James scored 21 points but had 6 turnovers. It was the first NBA title for Dallas.

LeBron James has gone from being one of the most popular NBA players to someone that most want to see lose. James did not help himself after Miami lost when he said, "All the people that was rooting on me to fail, at the end of the day they have to wake up tomorrow and have the same life that they had before they woke up today". To silence his critics, James will need to expand his skills by adding a post game and hit more outside shots, while Miami will need to find the right pieces to fit around him, Wade and Bosh, and they don't have the money to buy any more stars.

In Cleveland, the problem was that he didn't have the second superstar next to him. That has changed now with the Heat, where the problem is figuring out who is the number one option. James may need to change his game, and become the Pippen to Wade's Jordan. James at point guard, like Magic Johnson, could also work. Has LeBron James hit his peak as a player? What will the second half of his career bring? Will he win multiple titles like Jordan and Kobe, or will he be remembered as one of the greatest players to never win a championship, like Charles Barkley and Karl Malone? Only time will tell, but with rising stars such as Kevin Durant, Derrick Rose, and rookies like Blake Griffin raising their games, the road will certainly not get any easier.

About Minute Help Press

Minute Help Press is building a library of books for people with only minutes to spare. Follow @minutehelp on Twitter to receive the latest information about free and paid publications from Minute Help Press, or visit minutehelpguides.com.

CPSIA information can be obtained at www.ICGtesting.com
Printed in the USA
LVOW05s0958150115

422818LV00032B/751/P

9 781500 982331